Review
Counting Coins

Name

Date

To parents At first, your child will review the coins and their values. If your child encounters difficulty, you could show him or her real coins and review what they are worth.

■ Trace or write the amount that each coin is worth while saying it aloud.

Front		Back	
	1 ¢		¢
	5 ¢		¢
	10 ¢		¢
	25 ¢		¢
	50 ¢		¢

■ Write the amount that each coin is worth while saying it aloud.

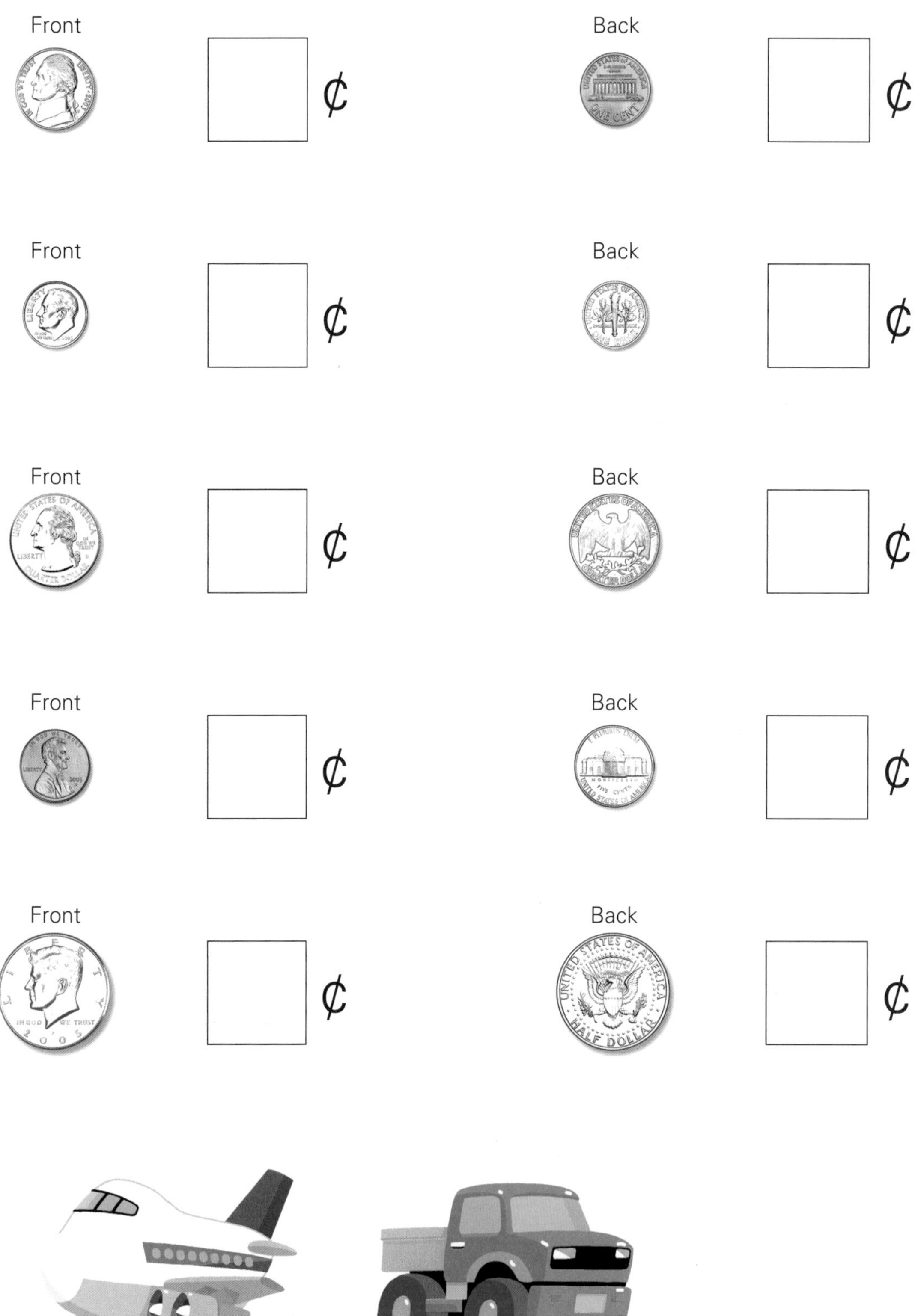

Review
Counting Coins

Name
Date

To parents In these review exercises, your child is asked to add together the money in each purse. You can help by counting along with him or her.

■ Add the value of the coins in each purse. Then write the amount in the box on the right.

7 ¢

¢

¢

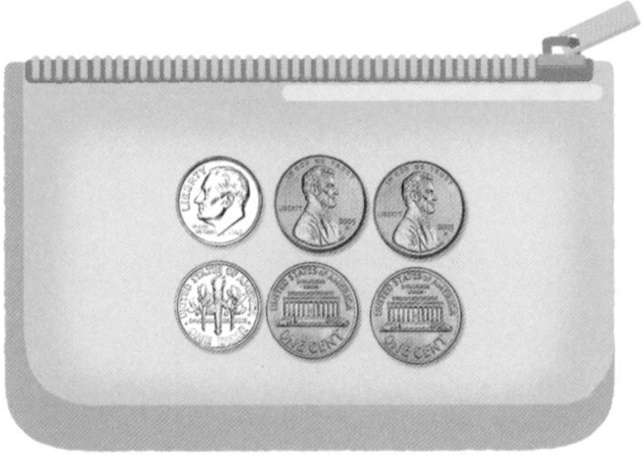

¢

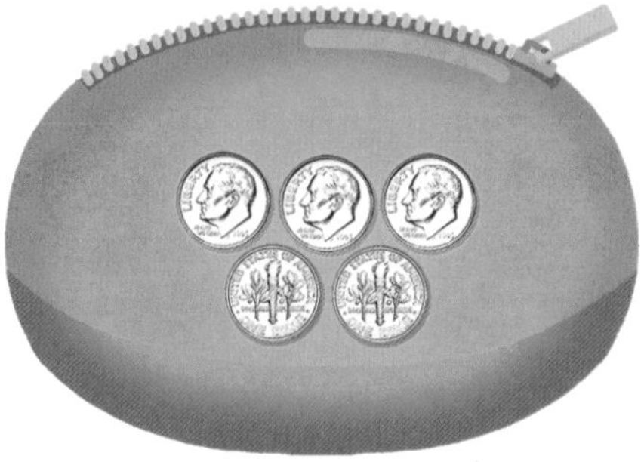

¢

¢

¢

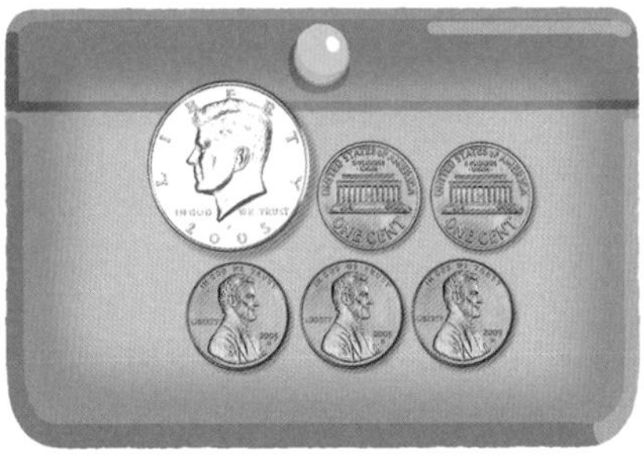

¢

■ Add the value of the coins in each purse. Then write the amount in the box on the right.

3 Counting Coins
To 100 Cents

Name
Date

■ Add the value of each row of coins. Then write the amount on the right.

(1)  90 ¢

(2)  ¢

(3)  ¢

(4)  ¢

(5)  75 ¢

(6)  ¢

(7)  ¢

(8)  ¢

(9)  ¢

(10)  ¢

■ Add the value of each row of coins. Then write the amount on the right.

(1) 50 ¢

(2) ¢

(3) ¢

(4) ¢

(5) ¢

(6) ¢

(7) ¢

(8) ¢

(9) ¢

(10) ¢

4 Counting Coins
To 100 Cents

Name

Date

■ Add the value of each group of coins. Then trace the amount on the right.

①  80 ¢

②   90 ¢

③   90 ¢

④  95 ¢

⑤  99 ¢

⑥  100 ¢

⑦   100 ¢

⑧  100 ¢

⑨  100 ¢

⑩ 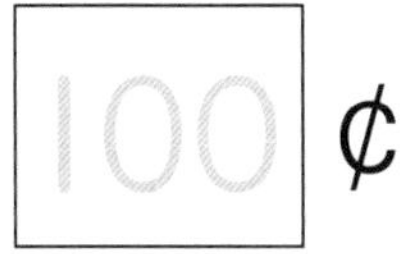 100 ¢

■ Add the value of each group of coins. Then write the amount on the right.

(1) 100¢

(2) ☐ ¢

(3) ☐ ¢

(4) 100¢

(5) ☐ ¢

(6) 100¢

(7) ☐ ¢

(8) ☐ ¢

(9) ☐ ¢

(10) 100 ¢

5 Counting Coins
100 Cents

Name
Date

To parents The fact that 100 cents equals a dollar is a very difficult concept for children to understand. Try thinking of some recent purchases that cost a dollar, and illustrate different ways to come up with that amount with real coins.

100¢ = $1 (100 cents is 1 dollar)

■ Add the value of each row of coins. Then write the amount on the right.

①  100¢ → $ 1

②  ☐ ¢

③  ☐ ¢

④  100¢ → $ 1

⑤  ☐ ¢

⑥  100¢ → $ 1

⑦  ☐ ¢

⑧  ☐ ¢

■ Add the value of each row of coins. Then trace or write the amount on the right.

(1)  [ ] ¢

(2)  [ ] ¢

(3)  [100] ¢ → $ [1]

(4)  [100] ¢ → $ [1]

(5)  [ ] ¢

(6)  [ ] ¢

(7)  [ ] ¢

(8)  [ ] ¢

(9)  [100] ¢ → $ [1]

(10)  [ ] ¢

6 Counting Coins

100 Cents

Name

Date

Add the value of each row of coins. Then trace or write the amount on the right.

①
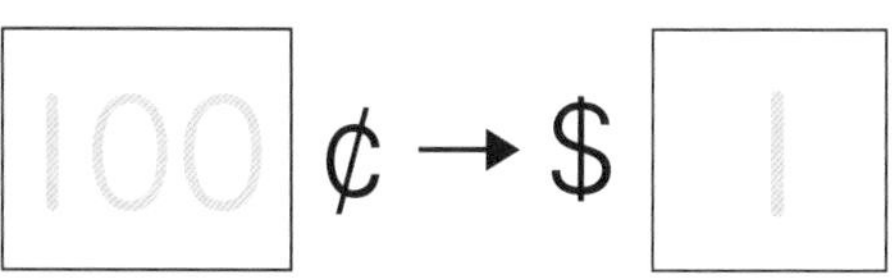
100 ¢ → $ 1

② 
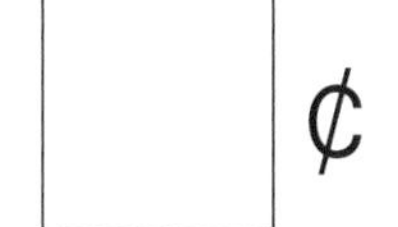
¢

③ 
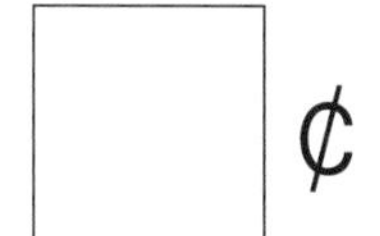
¢

④ 
100 ¢ → $ 1

⑤ 
¢

⑥ ¢

⑦ 
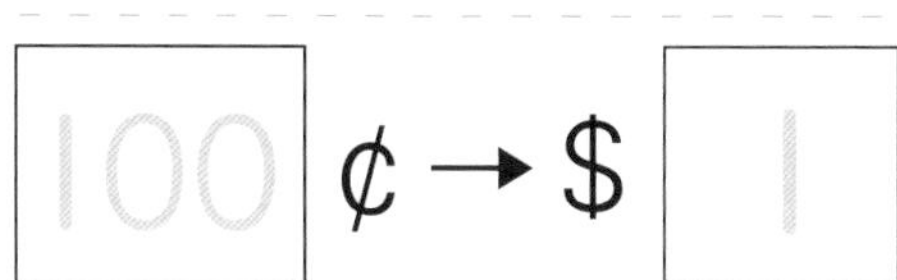
100 ¢ → $ 1

⑧ 
¢

⑨ ¢

⑩ 100 ¢ → $ 1

■ Add the value of each row of coins. Then trace or write the amount on the right.

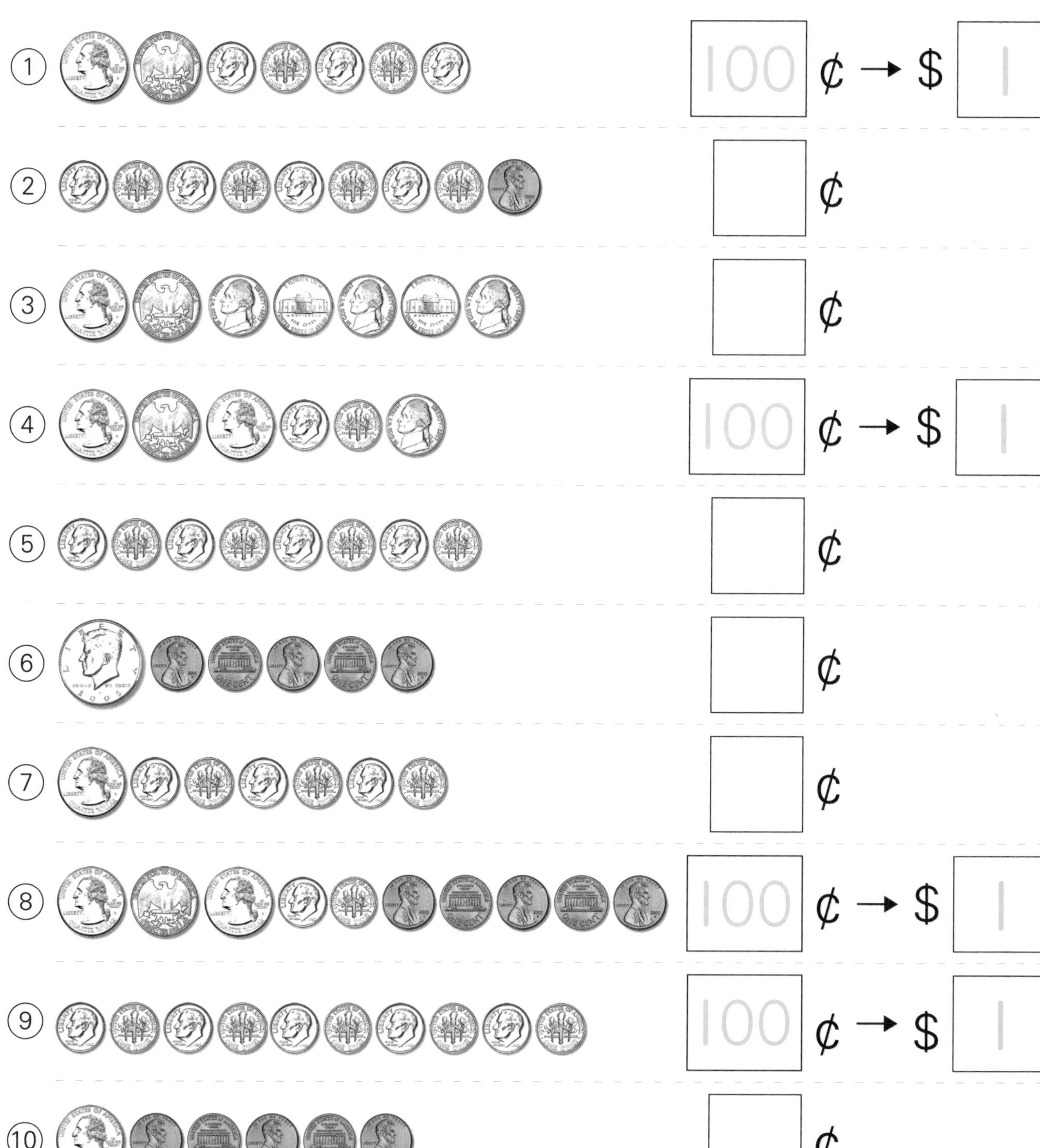

(1) 100 ¢ → $ 1

(2) ¢

(3) ¢

(4) 100 ¢ → $ 1

(5) ¢

(6) ¢

(7) ¢

(8) 100 ¢ → $ 1

(9) 100 ¢ → $ 1

(10) ¢

7 Counting Coins
100 Cents

Name
Date

■ Add the value of each group of coins. Then trace or write the amount on the right.

①  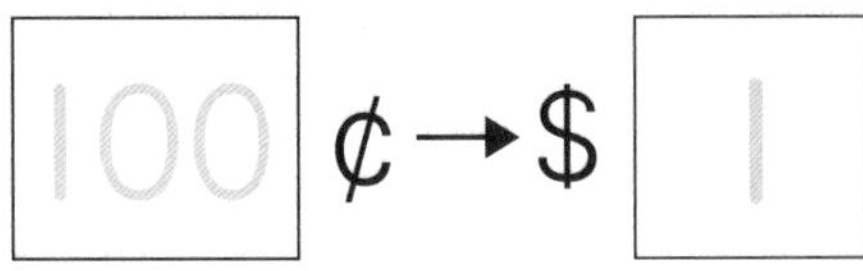 100 ¢ → $ 1

②   ¢

③   ¢

④  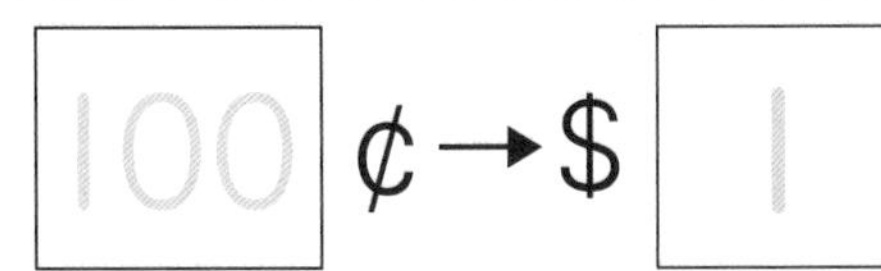 100 ¢ → $ 1

⑤   ¢

⑥  ¢

⑦  100 ¢ → $ 1

⑧   ¢

⑨   ¢

⑩ 100 ¢ → $ 1

Add the value of each group of coins. Then trace or write the amount on the right.

①  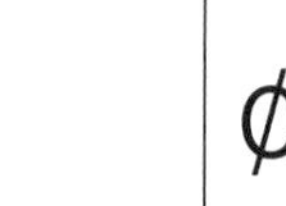

②  

③  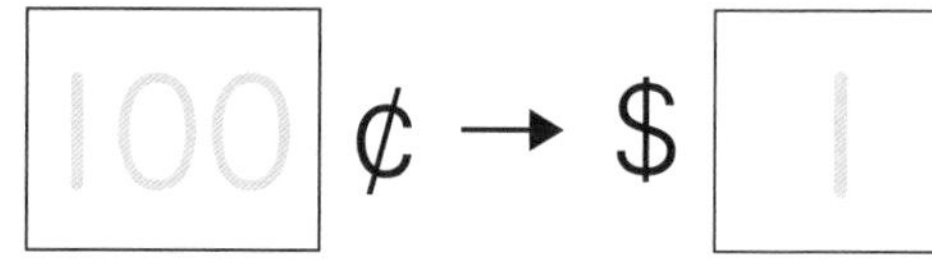

④  

⑤  100 ¢ → $ 1

⑥  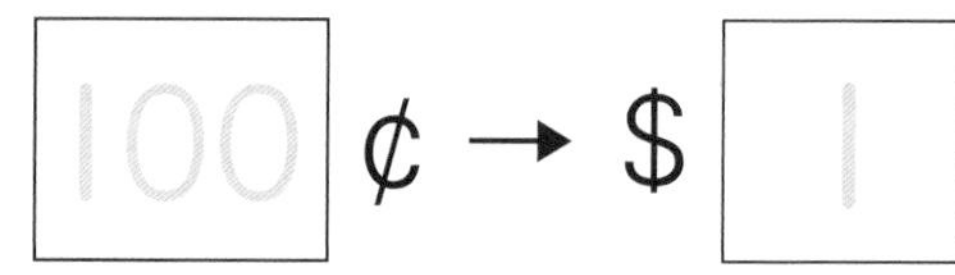

⑦  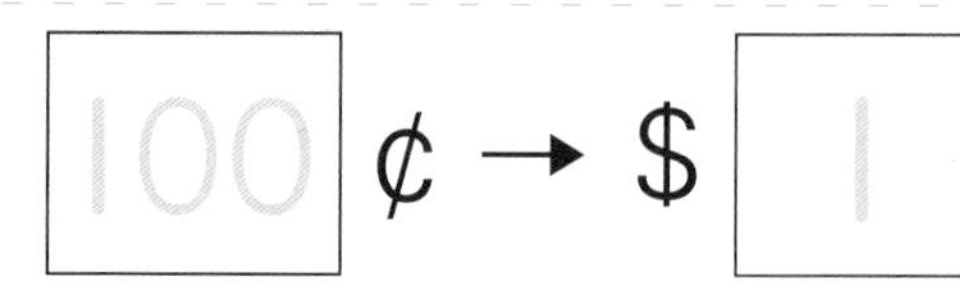

⑧  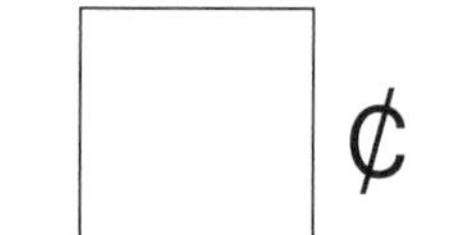

⑨  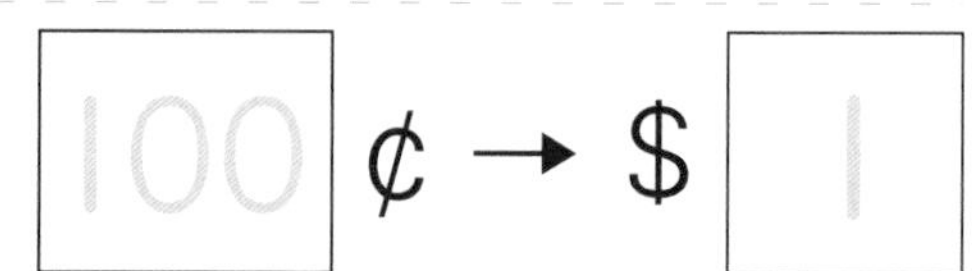

⑩  100 ¢ → $ 1

8 Counting Coins
1 Dollar

Name
Date

■ Add the value of each group of coins. Then write the amount on the right.

①  $ 1

②  $

③  $

④  $

⑤  $

⑥  $

⑦  $

⑧  $

⑨  $

⑩  $

■ Add the value of each group of coins. Then write the amount on the right.

(1) $ 1

(2) $

(3) $

(4) $

(5) $

(6) $

(7) $

(8) $

(9) $

(10) $

9 Counting Money
1 Dollar

Name
Date

To parents On this page, your child will first encounter the dollar bill. Point out the different symbol, and the different names for dollars and cents, to help your child understand the difference.

■ Count the money in each pair of hands. Then write the amount in the box on the right.

$1 Front Back

① $ □ $ □

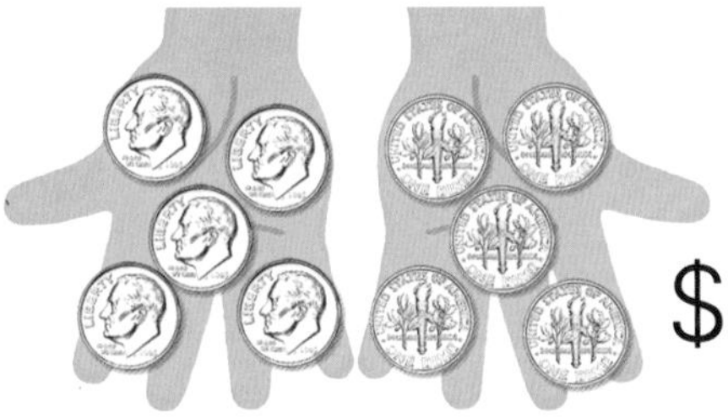

② $ □ $ □

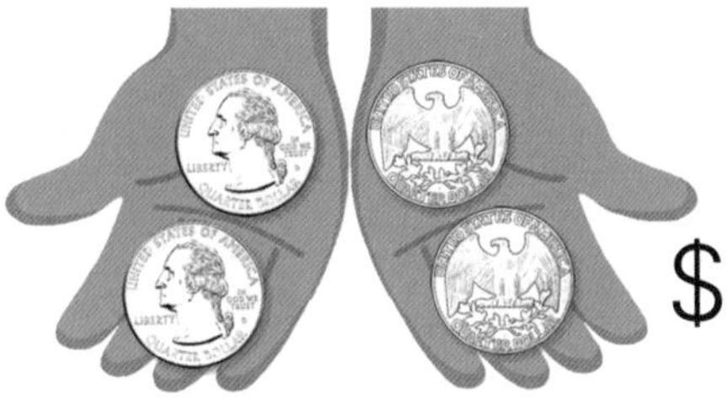

③ $ □ $ □

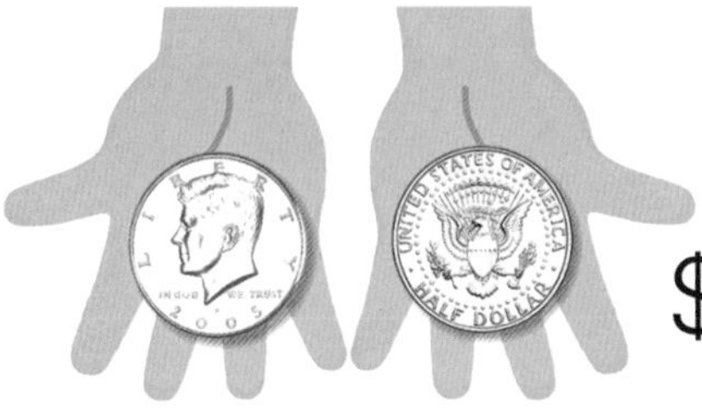

④ $ □ $ □

■ Count the money in each pair of hands. Then write the amount in the box on the right.

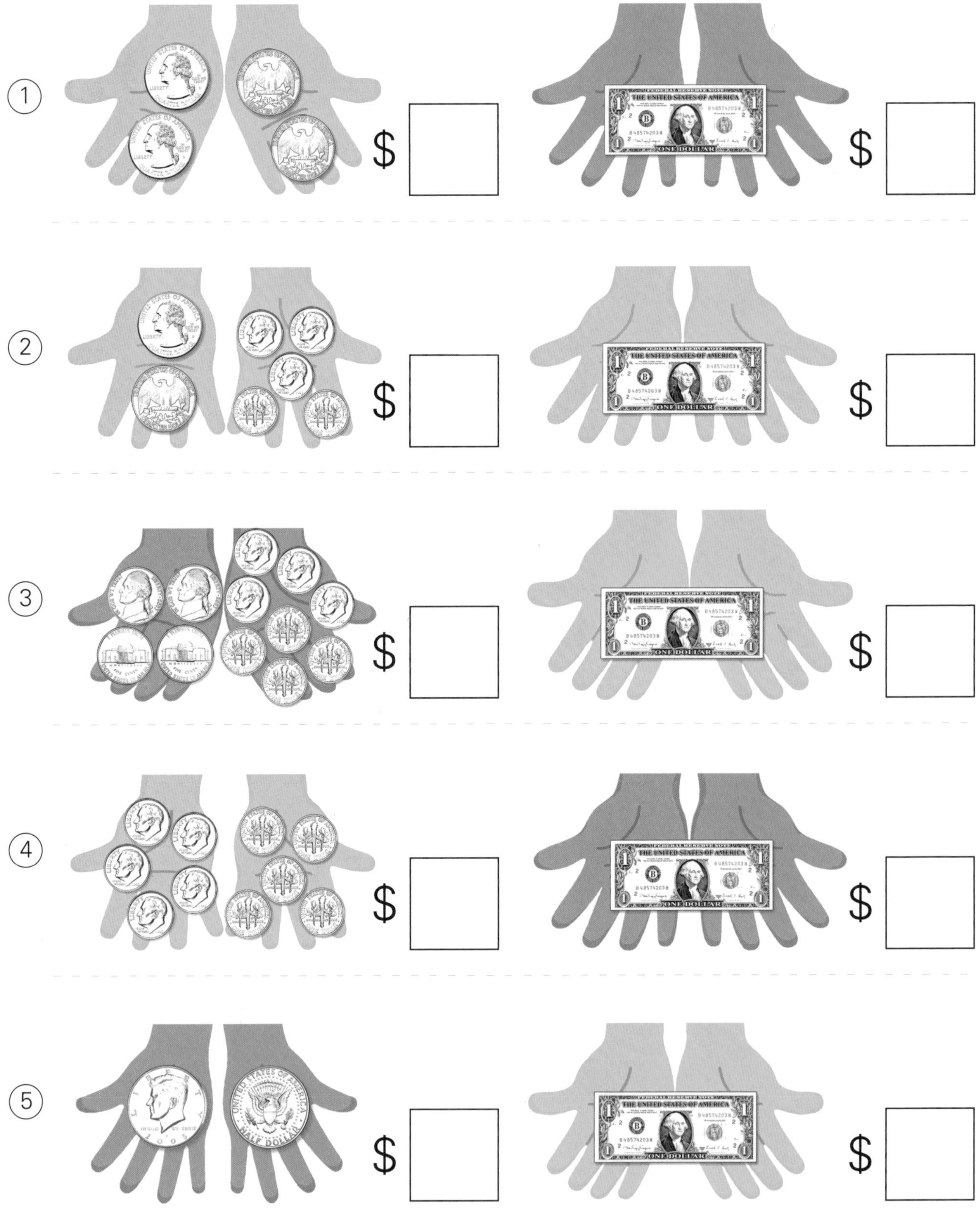

10 Counting Money
Dollars and Cents

Name

Date

■ Count the money in each row. Then trace or write the amount on the right.

(1)		$1
(2)		$1 and 1 ¢
(3)		$1 and 2 ¢
(4)		$1 and ☐ ¢
(5)		$1 and ☐ ¢
(6)		$1 and ☐ ¢
(7)		$1 and 5 ¢
(8)		$1 and 10 ¢
(9)		$1 and 25 ¢
(10)		$1 and 50 ¢

■ Count the money in each row. Then write the amount on the right.

(1) $1 and ☐ ¢

(2) $1 and ☐ ¢

(3) $1 and ☐ ¢

(4) $1 and ☐ ¢

(5) $1 and ☐ ¢

(6) $1 and ☐ ¢

(7) $1 and ☐ ¢

(8) $1 and ☐ ¢

(9) $1 and ☐ ¢

Counting Money

Dollars and Cents

Name

Date

To parents Here, your child is introduced to a new way of writing monetary amounts. Please point out that all three columns have the same value. If your child encounters difficulty, try showing him or her a receipt or price tag so that he or she can see the real-world application of this concept.

■ Count the money in each row. Then trace the amount on the right.

① $1 → $1.00

②   $1 and 1¢ → $  1.01

③   $1 and 2¢ → $  1.02

④   $1 and 3¢ → $  1.03

⑤   $1 and 4¢ → $  1.04

⑥   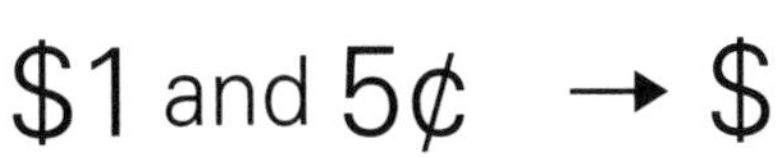 $1 and 5¢ → $  1.05

⑦   $1 and 5¢ → $  1.05

⑧    $1 and 10¢ → $  1.10

⑨    $1 and 25¢ → $  1.25

⑩   $1 and 50¢ → $ 1.50

■ Count the money in each row. Then write the amount on the right.

①  $1 → $1.00

②   $1 and 1¢ → $ 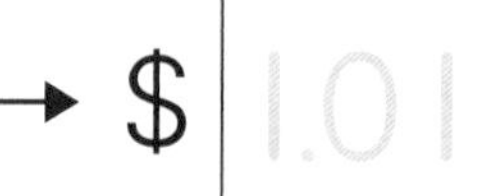

③   $1 and 2¢ → $ 

④   $1 and 3¢ → $ 

⑤   $1 and 4¢ → $ 

⑥   $1 and 5¢ → $ 

⑦   $1 and 5¢ → $ 

⑧   $1 and 10¢ → $ ☐

⑨   $1 and 25¢ → $ ☐

   $1 and 50¢ → $ ☐

12 Counting Money
Dollars and Cents

Name

Date

■ Count the money in each row. Then write the amount on the right.

①   $1 and 5¢ → $ 

②   $1 and 10¢ → $ ☐

③   $1 and 15¢ → $ ☐

④  $1 and 20¢ → $ ☐

⑤   $1 and 25¢ → $ ☐

⑥   $1 and 10¢ → $ ☐

⑦   $1 and 20¢ → $ ☐

⑧   $1 and 30¢ → $ ☐

⑨   $1 and 25¢ → $ ☐

⑩  $1 and 50¢ → $ ☐

■ Count the money in each row. Then write the amount on the right.

①   $1 and 6¢ → $ 1.06

②   $1 and 12¢ → $ ☐

③   $1 and 15¢ → $ ☐

④   $1 and 35¢ → $ ☐

⑤   $1 and 21¢ → $ ☐

⑥   $1 and 27¢ → $ ☐

⑦   $1 and 20¢ → $ ☐

⑧   $1 and 16¢ → $ ☐

⑨   $1 and 35¢ → $ ☐

⑩   $1 and 80¢ → $ ☐

13 Counting Money

Dollars and Pennies

Name
Date

■ Count the money in each row. Then trace the amount on the right.

① $ 

②  $ 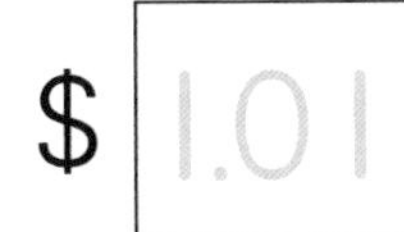

③  $ 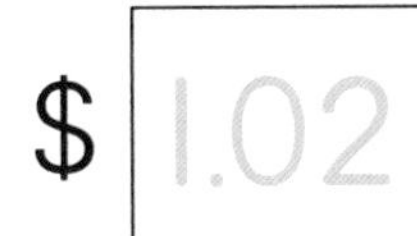

④  $ 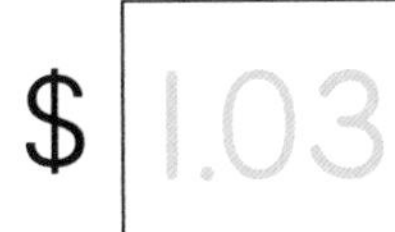

⑤  $ 

⑥  $ 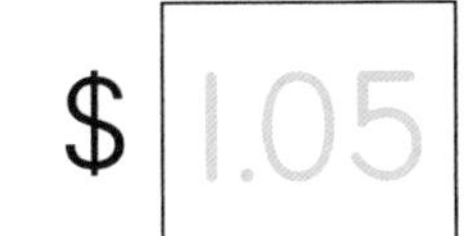

⑦ $ 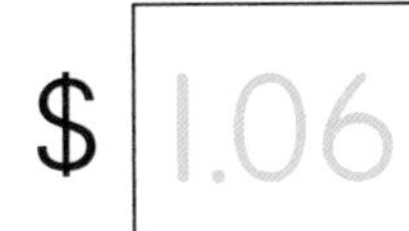

⑧  $ 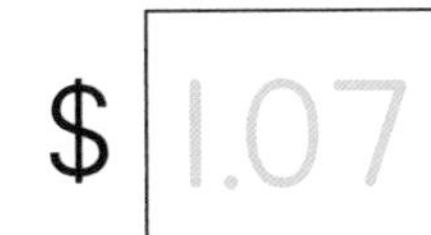

⑨  $ 1.08

⑩  $ 1.09

⑪  $ 1.10

■ Count the money in each row. Then write the amount on the right.

(1) $ 1.01

(2) $

(3) $

(4) $

(5) $

(6) $

(7) $

(8) $

(9) $

(10) $

14 Counting Money
Dollars and Nickels

Name

Date

■ Count the money in each row. Then trace the amount on the right.

(1)  $ 1.05

(2)  $ 1.10

(3)  $ 1.15

(4)  $ 1.20

(5)  $ 1.25

(6)  $ 1.30

(7)  $ 1.35

(8)  $ 1.40

(9)  $ 1.45

(10)  $ 1.50

■ Count the money in each row. Then write the amount on the right.

(1) $ 1.05

(2) $

(3) $

(4) $

(5) $

(6) $

(7) $

(8) $

(9) $

(10) $

15 Counting Money
Dollars and Dimes

Name

Date

■ Count the money in each row. Then trace the amount on the right.

(1)  $ 1.10

(2)  $ 1.20

(3)  $ 1.30

(4)  $ 1.40

(5)  $ 1.50

(6)  $ 1.60

(7)  $ 1.70

(8)  $ 1.80

(9)  $ 1.90

(10)  $ 2.00

■ Count the money in each row. Then write the amount on the right.

①  $ 1.10

②  $

③  $

④  $

⑤  $

⑥  $

⑦  $

⑧  $

⑨  $

⑩  $

16 Counting Money

Dollars, Half Dollars and Quarters

Name

Date

■ Count the money in each row. Then trace the amount on the right.

①  $ 

②   $ 

③   $ 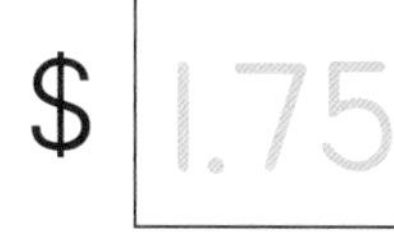

④   $ 

⑤   $ 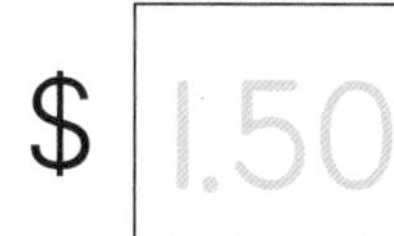

■ Count the money in each row. Then write the amount on the right.

①   $ 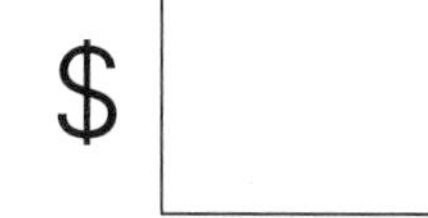

②   $ 

③   $ 

④   $ 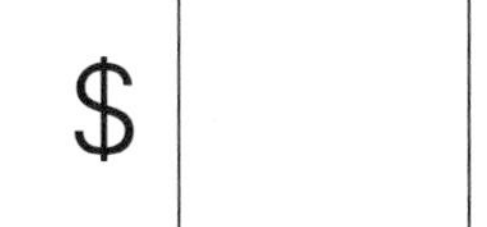

⑤   $ 

■ Count the money in each row. Then write the amount on the right.

(1) $ 1.01

(2) $

(3) $

(4) $

(5) $

(6) $

(7) $

(8) $

(9) $

(10) $

Review

Name
Date

■ Count the money in each piggy bank. Then write the amount in the box on the right.

$ 1.02

$

$

$

$

$

$

$

■ Count the money in each piggy bank. Then write the amount in the box on the right.

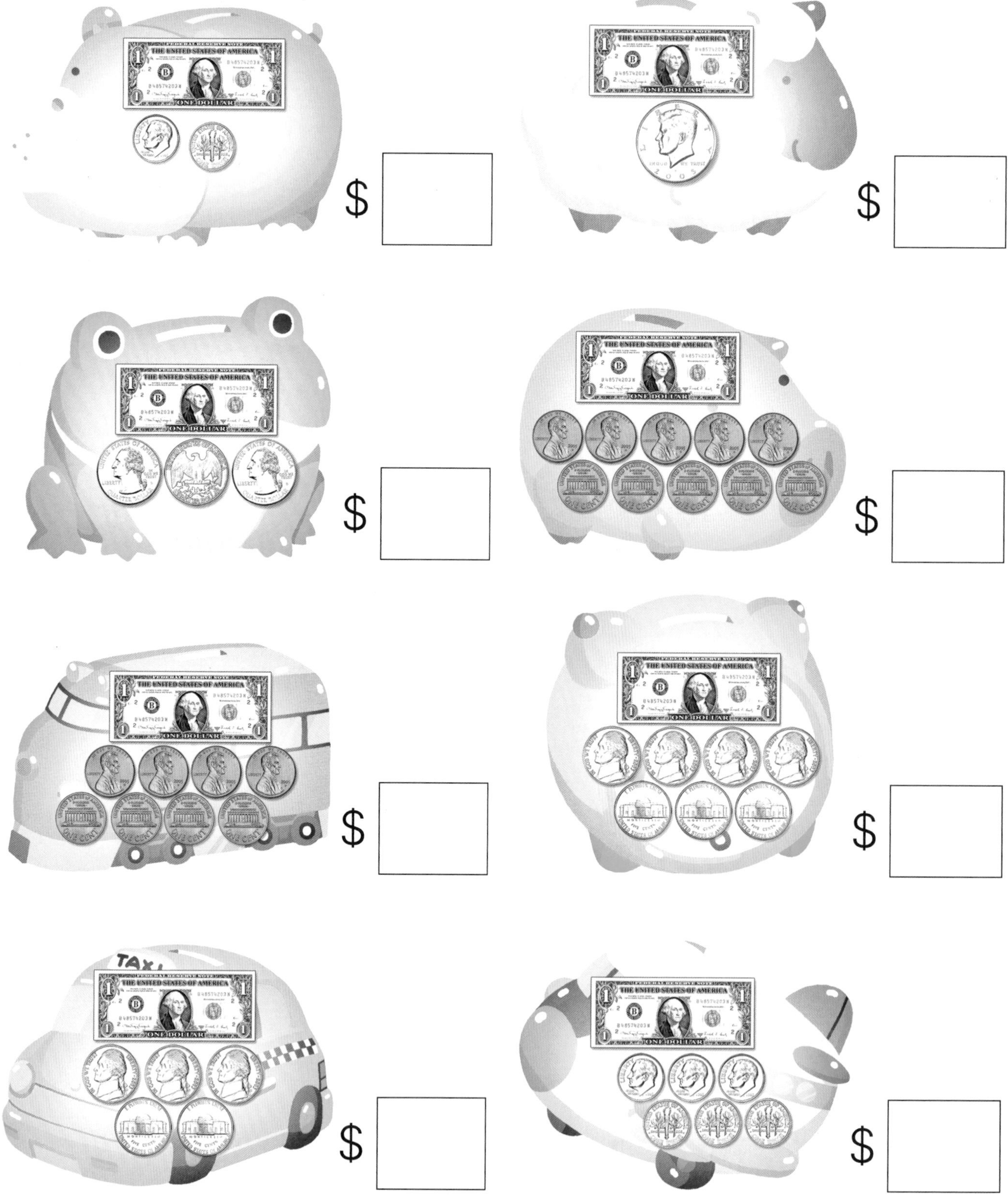

18 Counting Money
Dollars, Nickels and Pennies

Name

Date

■ Count the money in each row. Then trace the amount on the right.

①  $ 1.06

②  $ 1.07

③  $ 1.08

④  $ 1.09

⑤  $ 1.10

⑥  $ 1.11

⑦  $ 1.12

⑧  $ 1.13

⑨  $ 1.14

⑩  $ 1.15

■ Count the money in each row. Then write the amount on the right.

(1) $ 1.06

(2) $

(3) $

(4) $

(5) $

(6) $

(7) $

(8) $

(9) $

(10) $

19 Counting Money
Dollars, Dimes and Pennies

Name

Date

■ Count the money in each row. Then trace the amount on the right.

①  $ 1.11

②  $ 1.12

③  $ 1.13

④  $ 1.14

⑤  $ 1.15

⑥  $ 1.21

⑦  $ 1.22

⑧  $ 1.23

⑨  $ 1.24

⑩  $ 1.25

■ Count the money in each row. Then write the amount on the right.

①  $ 1.11

②  $

③  $

④  $

⑤  $

⑥  $

⑦  $

⑧  $

⑨  $

⑩  $

20 Counting Money

Dollars, Quarters and Pennies

Name

Date

■ Count the money in each row. Then trace the amount on the right.

①  $  1.26

②   $  1.27

③   $ 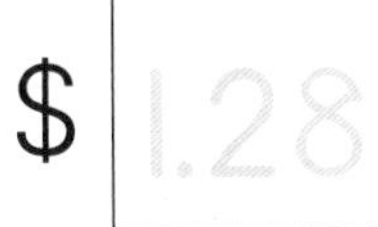 1.28

④   $  1.29

⑤   $  1.30

⑥   $ 1.51

⑦   $ 1.52

⑧   $ 1.53

⑨   $ 1.54

⑩   $ 1.55

■ Count the money in each row. Then write the amount on the right.

①  $ 1.28

②  $

③  $

④  $

⑤  $

⑥  $

⑦  $

⑧  $

⑨  $

⑩  $

21 Counting Money

Dollars, Half Dollars, Quarters and Pennies

Name
Date

■ Count the money in each row. Then trace the amount on the right.

1.  $ 1.76
2.  $ 1.77
3.  $ 1.78
4.  $ 1.79
5.  $ 1.80
6.  $ 1.51
7.  $ 1.52
8.  $ 1.53
9.  $ 1.54
10.  $ 1.55

■ Count the money in each row. Then write the amount on the right.

1. $ 1.76
2. $
3. $
4. $
5. $
6. $
7. $
8. $
9. $
10. $

Review
How Much?

Name
Date

■ Count the money in each wallet. Then write the amount in the box on the right.

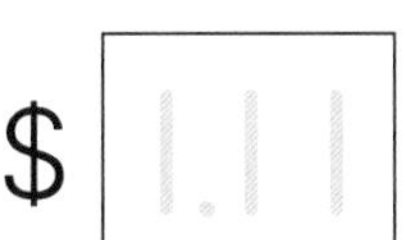

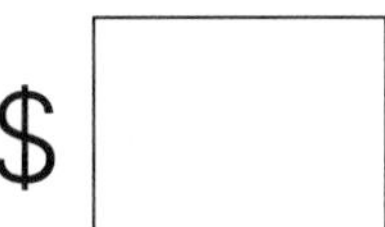

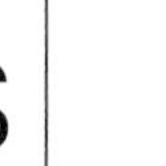

$

$

$

$

■ Count the money in each wallet. Then write the amount in the box on the right.

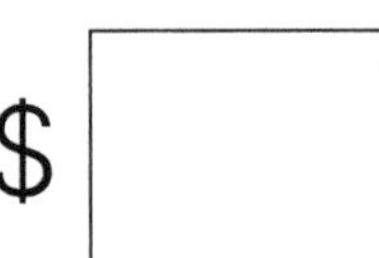

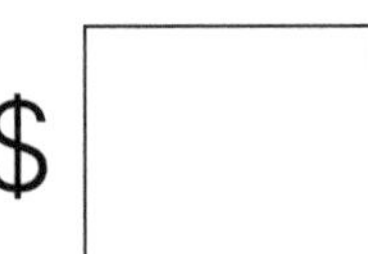

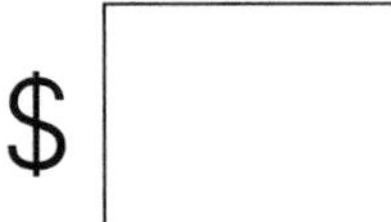

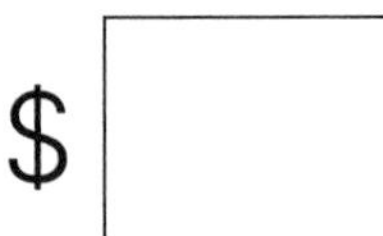

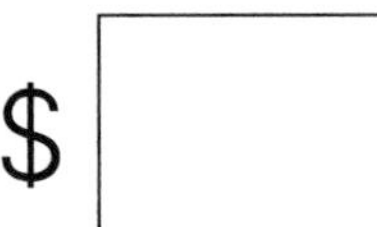

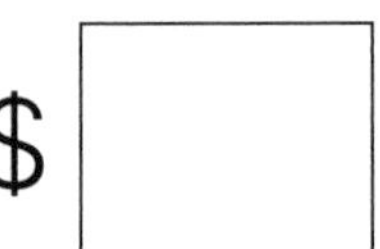

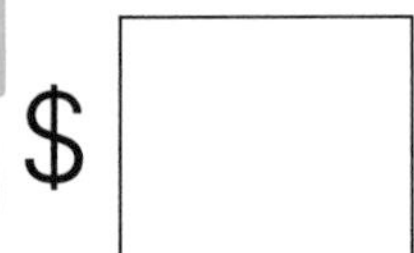

23 Counting Money

Dollars, Dimes and Nickels

Name

Date

■ Count the money in each row. Then trace the amount on the right.

①  $ 

②   $ 

③   $ 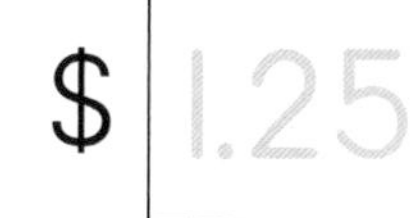

④   $ 

⑤   $ 

⑥   $ 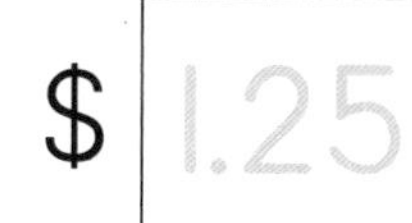

⑦   $ 

⑧   $ 1.35

⑨   $ 1.40

⑩   $ 1.45

■ Count the money in each row. Then write the amount on the right.

(1) $ 1.15

(2) $ ☐

(3) $ ☐

(4) $ ☐

(5) $ ☐

(6) $ ☐

(7) $ ☐

(8) $ ☐

(9) $ ☐

(10) $ ☐

24 Counting Money

Dollars, Quarters and Nickels

Name

Date

■ Count the money in each row. Then trace the amount on the right.

① 
$ 

②  
$ 

③  
$ 

④  
$ 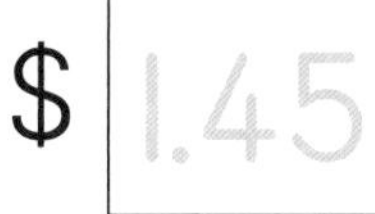

⑤  
$ 

⑥  
$ 

⑦  
$ 

⑧  
$ 1.65

⑨  
$ 1.70

⑩     
$ 

■ Count the money in each row. Then write the amount on the right.

①  $ 1.30

② $

③ $

④ $

⑤ $

⑥ $

⑦ $

⑧ $

⑨ $

⑩ $

25 Counting Money

Dollars, Half Dollars, Dimes and Nickels

Name
Date

■ Count the money in each row. Then trace the amount on the right.

(1) $ 1.55

(2) $ 1.60

(3) $ 1.65

(4) $ 1.70

(5) $ 1.75

(6) $ 1.60

(7) $ 1.70

(8) $ 1.80

(9) $ 1.90

(10) $ 2.00

■ Count the money in each row. Then write the amount on the right.

1. $ 1.55
2. $
3. $
4. $
5. $
6. $
7. $
8. $
9. $
10. $

Review
How Much?

Name

Date

■ Count the money in each box. Then write the amount in the box on the right.

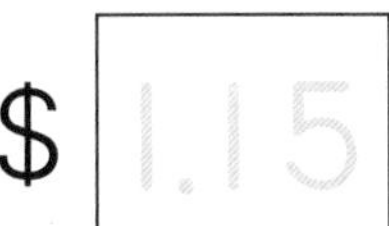

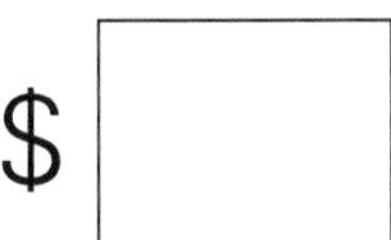

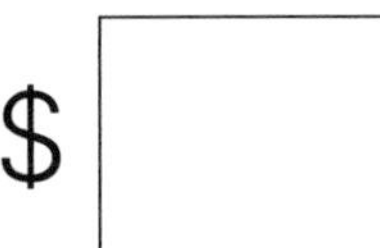

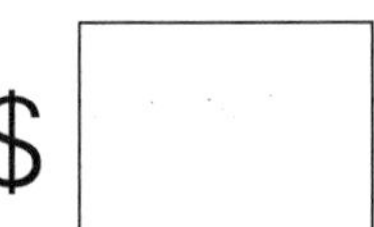

$

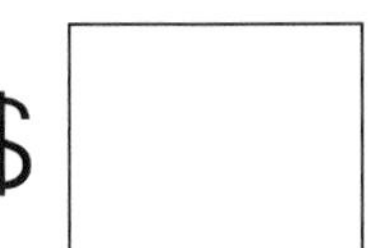

$

$

■ Count the money in each box. Then write the amount in the box on the right.

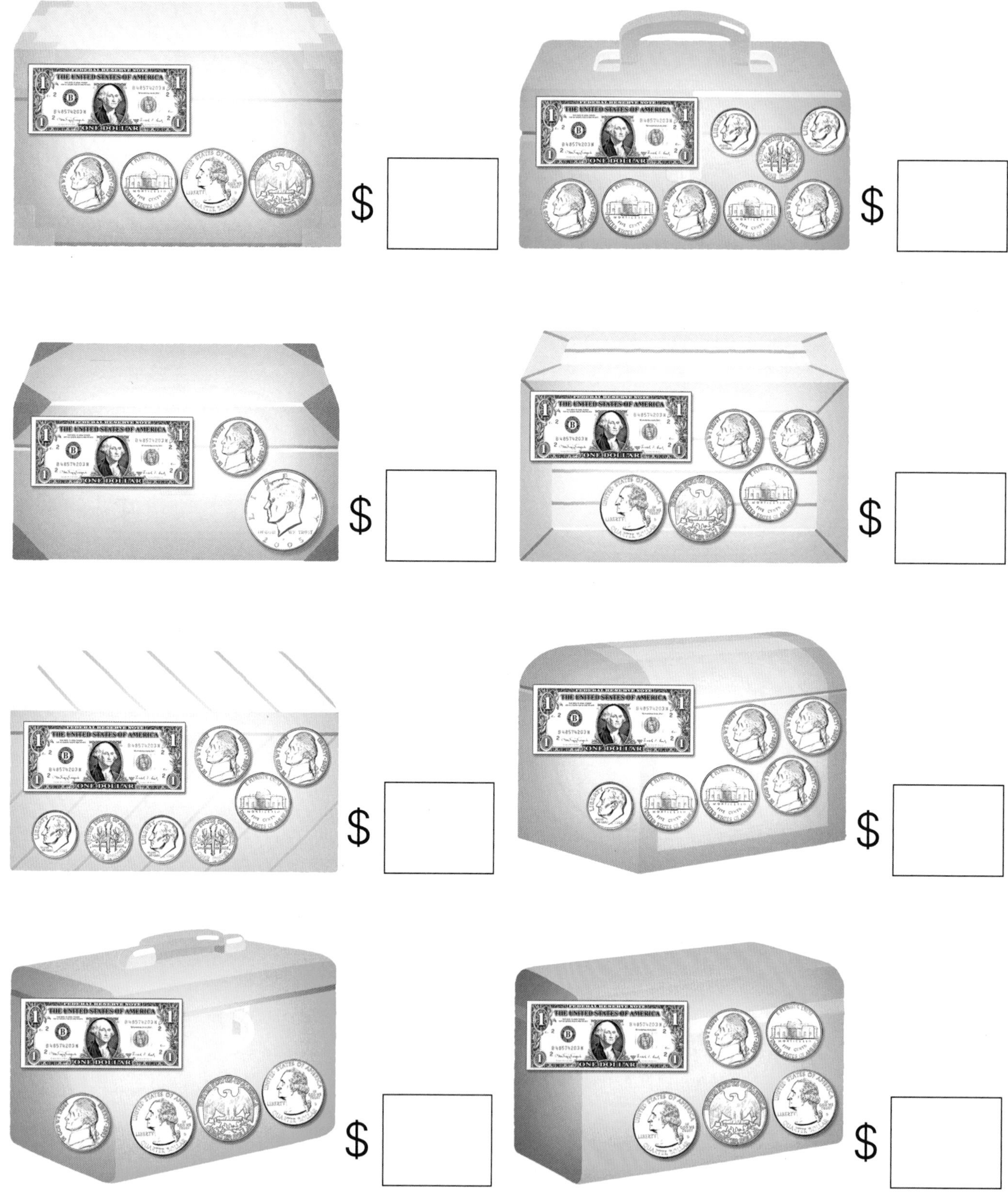

Counting Money

Dollars, Dimes, Nickels and Pennies

Name

Date

■ Count the money in each row. Then trace the amount on the right.

① $ 1.16

② $ 1.17

③ $ 1.18

④ $ 1.19

⑤ $ 1.20

⑥ $ 1.26

⑦ $ 1.27

⑧ $ 1.28

⑨ $ 1.29

⑩ $ 1.30

■ Count the money in each row. Then write the amount on the right.

1. \$ 1.16

2. \$

3. \$

4. \$

5. \$

6. \$

7. \$

8. \$

9. \$

10. \$

Counting Money

Dollars, Quarters, Nickels and Pennies

Name
Date

■ Count the money in each row. Then trace the amount on the right.

1. $ 1.31
2. $ 1.32
3. $ 1.33
4. $ 1.34
5. $ 1.35
6. $ 1.56
7. $ 1.57
8. $ 1.58
9. $ 1.59
10. $ 1.60

■ Count the money in each row. Then write the amount on the right.

①  $ 1.31

②  $

③  $

④  $

⑤  $

⑥  $

⑦  $

⑧  $

⑨  $

⑩  $

29 Counting Money

Dollars, Quarters, Dimes and Pennies

Name

Date

■ Count the money in each row. Then trace the amount on the right.

(1) $ 1.36

(2) $ 1.37

(3) $ 1.38

(4) $ 1.39

(5) $ 1.40

(6) $ 1.61

(7) $ 1.62

(8) $ 1.63

(9) $ 1.64

(10) $ 1.65

■ Count the money in each row. Then write the amount on the right.

(1) $ 1.36

(2) $

(3) $

(4) $

(5) $

(6) $

(7) $

(8) $

(9) $

(10) $

30 Counting Money

Dollars, Quarters, Dimes and Nickels

Name

Date

■ Count the money in each row. Then trace the amount on the right.

(1)  $ 1.40

(2)  $ 1.45

(3)  $ 1.50

(4)  $ 1.55

(5)  $ 1.60

(6)  $ 1.65

(7)  $ 1.70

(8)  $ 1.75

(9)  $ 1.80

(10)  $ 1.85

■ Count the money in each row. Then write the amount on the right.

1. $ 1.40
2. $
3. $
4. $
5. $
6. $
7. $
8. $
9. $
10. $

31 Counting Money

Dollars, Quarters, Dimes, Nickels and Pennies

Name
Date

■ Count the money in each row. Then trace the amount on the right.

(1)  $ 1.41

(2)  $ 1.42

(3)  $ 1.43

(4)  $ 1.44

(5)  $ 1.45

(6)  $ 1.51

(7)  $ 1.52

(8)  $ 1.53

(9)  $ 1.54

(10)  $ 1.55

■ Count the money in each row. Then write the amount on the right.

①  $ 1.41

②  $

③  $

④  $

⑤  $

⑥  $

⑦  $

⑧  $

⑨  $

⑩  $

32 Review
How Much?

Name	
Date	

■ Count the money in each pair of hands. Then write the amount in the box on the right.

$ ______ $ ______

$ ______ $ ______

$ ______ $ ______

$ ______ $ ______

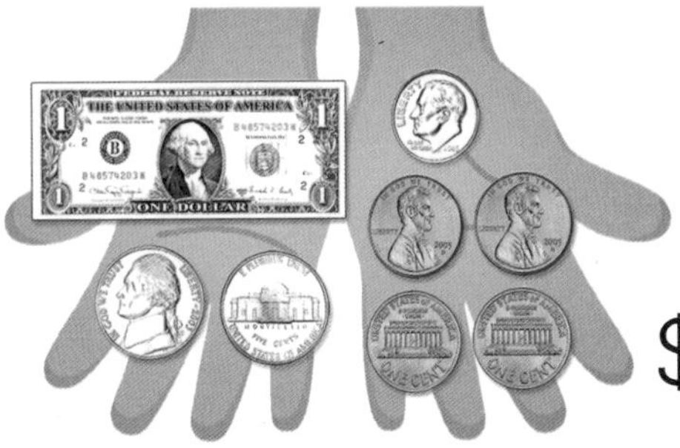

■ Count the money in each pair of hands. Then write the amount in the box on the right.

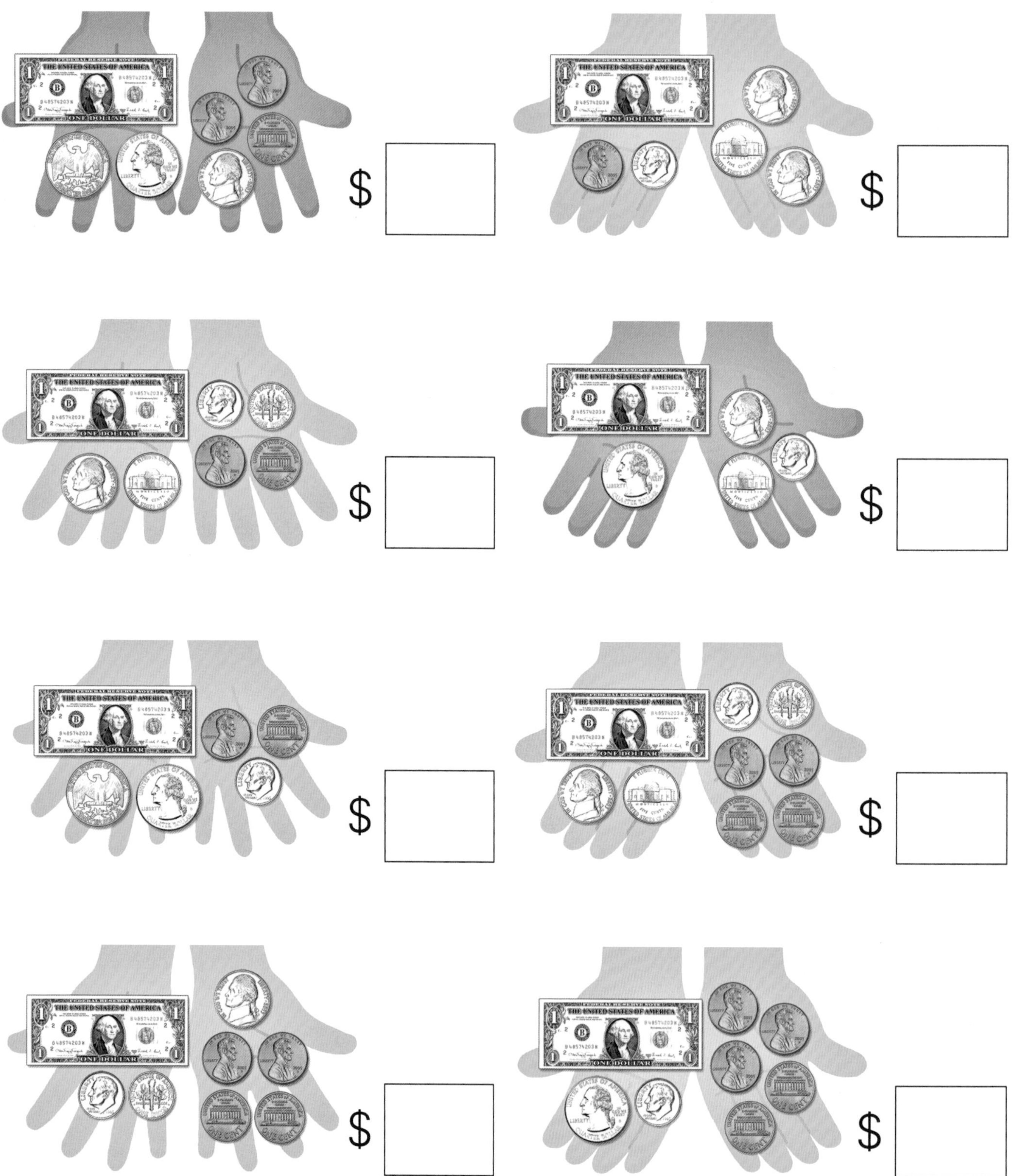

33 Exchange Unit

From ¢ to $

Name

Date

To parents On this page, your child will practice going from cents to dollars. It might help to get a receipt out in order to help your child see the decimal notation.

■ Add the value of each row of coins. Then trace the amount on the right.

①  100¢ → $ 1.00

② 90¢ → $ 0.90

③ 80¢ → $ 0.80

④ 70¢ → $ 0.70

⑤ 60¢ → $ 0.60

⑥ 50¢ → $ 0.50

⑦ 40¢ → $ 0.40

⑧ 30¢ → $ 0.30

⑨ 20¢ → $ 0.20

⑩ 10¢ → $ 0.10

■ Add the value of each row of coins. Then write the amount on the right.

①  100¢ → $ [ ]

②  90¢ → $ [0.90]

③ 80¢ → $ [ ]

④ 70¢ → $ [ ]

⑤ 60¢ → $ [ ]

⑥ 50¢ → $ [ ]

⑦ 40¢ → $ [ ]

⑧ 30¢ → $ [ ]

⑨ 20¢ → $ [ ]

⑩ 10¢ → $ [ ]

Exchange Unit

From ¢ to $

Name

Date

■ Add the value of each row of coins. Then write the amount on the right.

① 10¢ → $ 0.10

②  20¢ → $

③  30¢ → $

④  40¢ → $

⑤  50¢ → $

⑥  60¢ → $

⑦  70¢ → $

⑧  80¢ → $

⑨  90¢ → $

⑩  100¢ → $

■ Add the value of each row of coins. Then write the amount on the right.

(1)  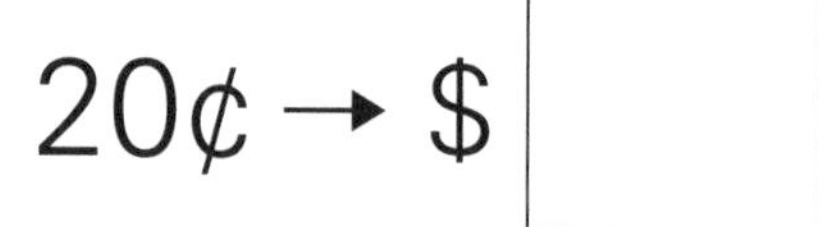

(2)  30¢ → $ ☐

(3) 40¢ → $ ☐

(4) 60¢ → $ ☐

(5) 70¢ → $ ☐

(6) 80¢ → $ ☐

(7) 10¢ → $ ☐

(8) 90¢ → $ ☐

(9) 100¢ → $ ☐

(10) 50¢ → $ ☐

35 Counting Coins
To 100 Cents

Name
Date

■ Add the value of each row of coins. Then write the amount on the right.

(1) $ 1.00

(2) $

(3) $

(4) $

(5) $

(6)  $

(7)  $

(8) $

(9) $

(10) $

■ Add the value of each row of coins. Then write the amount on the right.

① $ ☐

② $ ☐

③ $ ☐

④ $ ☐

⑤ $ ☐

⑥ $ ☐

⑦ $ ☐

⑧ $ ☐

⑨ $ ☐

⑩ $ ☐

36 Counting Coins

To 100 Cents

Name

Date

■ Add the value of each row of coins. Then trace the amount on the right.

① $  0.01

②  $  0.02

③  $  0.03

④  $  0.04

⑤  $ 0.05

⑥ $ 0.05

⑦  $ 0.10

⑧  $ 0.25

⑨  $ 0.50

⑩  $ 0.50

■ Add the value of each row of coins. Then write the amount on the right.

(1) $ ☐

(2) $ ☐

(3) $ ☐

(4) $ ☐

(5) $ ☐

(6) $ ☐

(7) $ ☐

(8) $ ☐

(9) $ ☐

(10) $ ☐

37 Comparing Money

Name

Date

To parents These exercises will help your child review the concepts he or she has learned in this book. Having real money on hand will help reinforce the idea that it's not always the side that has more coins that is worth more money.

■ Count the money in each row and write the amount on the right. Then circle the number that is larger.

(1)

$ 1.00

$ 0.80

(2)

$

$

(3)

$

$

(4)

$

$

(5)

$

$

■ Count the money in each row and write the amount on the right. Then circle the number that is larger.

(1)

$ ☐

$ ☐

(2)

$ ☐

$ ☐

(3)

$ ☐

$ ☐

(4)

$ ☐

$ ☐

(5)

$ ☐

$ ☐

38 Comparing Money

Name
Date

■Count the money in each row and write the amount on the right. Then circle the number that is larger.

① $ ☐

$ ☐

② $ ☐

$ ☐

③ $ ☐

$ ☐

④ $ ☐

$ ☐

⑤ $ ☐

$ ☐

■ Count the money in each row and write the amount on the right. Then circle the number that is larger.

1

$ ☐

$ ☐

2

$ ☐

$ ☐

3

$ ☐

$ ☐

4

$ ☐

$ ☐

5

$ ☐

$ ☐

39 Review

At the Store

Name

Date

■ Count the money needed to buy each toy. Write the price in dollars below.

$

$

$

$

$

$

■ Count the money needed to buy each treat. Write the price in dollars below.

Review
At the Store

Name

Date

To parents Has your child enjoyed learning about money? Hopefully this workbook has helped him or her develop real-world math skills. Offer your child congratulations!

■ Count the money needed to buy each piece of fruit. Write the price in dollars below.

$

$

$

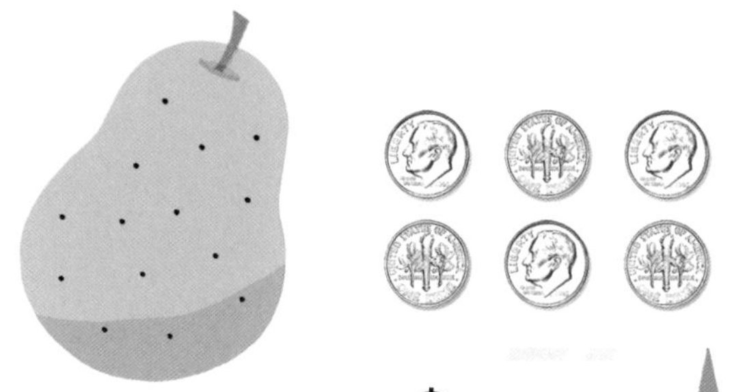

$

$

$

■ Count the money needed to buy each item. Write the price in dollars below.

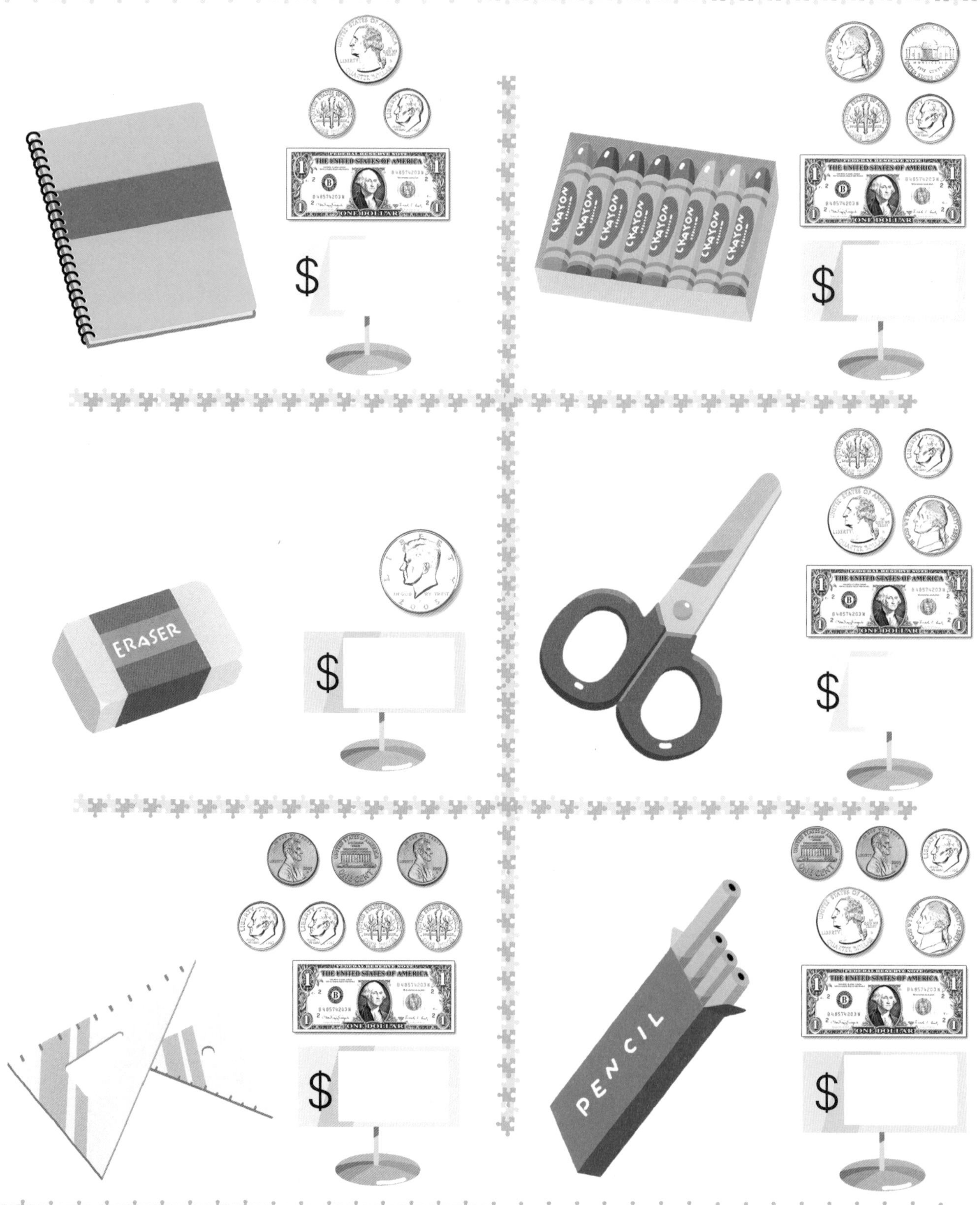

KUMON

Certificate of Achievement

____

is hereby congratulated on completing

My Book of Money: Dollars & Cents

Presented on ______________________________, 20____

____

Parent or Guardian